The Best 50

COOKIE RECIPES

Bristol Publishing

D0775805

BRISTOL PUBLISHING ENTERPRISES
Hayward, California

Printed in the United States of America.
ISBN 13: 978-1-55867-329-8

Cover design:	Frank J. Paredes
Cover photography:	John A. Benson
Food styling:	Randy Mon

THE GIFT OF GREAT COOKIES

For a snack, as a gift, for holidays and for special occasions: It's fun and easy to bake great cookies. However, it's important to remember a few guidelines that will help you make your cookies successful every time. Baking is more exact than other kinds of cooking: any change to your recipe will be more noticeable, and in some cases, will determine whether or not your cookies taste as good as they should. So read through the following tips before you begin to bake.

TIPS ON INGREDIENTS

- Using the correct amounts and types of ingredients is very important in baking. Substitutions can result in quite different-tasting cookies and, most importantly, may not bake correctly. When it comes to add-ins such as chocolate chips, nuts and dried fruit, however, substitution is usually fine. Try chocolate chips instead of raisins in oatmeal cookies, or add chopped dried apricots to chocolate chip cookies.

- Always pack brown sugar into the measuring cup or spoon.
- If a recipe simply lists "sugar" use white granulated sugar.
- These recipes are based on large eggs. Small, medium or extra-large eggs will change the dough and the cookies.
- To produce perfectly beaten egg whites, separate eggs while still cold from the fridge. Let whites warm to room temperature. Beat them in a completely clean glass, stainless or copper bowl with spotless beaters. (Plastic bowls tend to retain traces of grease even after washing.) Just a trace of fat —including egg yolk — will keep your whites from beating properly.
- If a recipe doesn't list a specific type of flour, use unbleached or all-purpose. Do not use cake flour unless specifically required; it's a softer product and will change the texture of your cookies.
- To add extra nutrition to your cookies, use half whole wheat

flour and half all-purpose flour. The cookies will be heavier, but will have added, nutty flavor.

- Generally speaking, butter will produce a thinner, crispy cookie and shortening will produce a thicker, chewier cookie.

- If you use a food processor to grind nuts for your recipes, add a little of the sugar or flour called for in the recipe to the nuts in the workbowl before you begin grinding. And don't over-process — you want ground nuts, not nut butter.

TIPS ON BAKING

- To avoid scorching chocolate, don't melt it over direct heat. Instead, place chopped chocolate or chocolate chips in the top of a double boiler (or in a bowl), uncovered, over hot water on low heat, stirring often. Or put the chocolate in a microwave-safe dish and microwave, uncovered, on high power. Check and stir every 30 seconds. Make sure no liquid comes in contact with the chocolate, or it will seize up. Butter and whipping cream are fine, though, as they contain large amounts of fat.

- Use a cookie sheet that's the right size for your oven: Allow at least 2 inches around all sides so hot air can circulate around the dough, producing more evenly baked cookies.
- If the cookie dough contains a lot of butter or margarine, you don't have to grease the cookie sheets. You can always line cookie sheets with parchment paper, which not only makes the cookies easy to remove, but makes cleanup a breeze.
- Always preheat your oven to the designated temperature well before you are ready to bake.
- It's best to bake one sheet of cookies at a time, on the center rack of your oven.
- Check cookies several minutes before the end of baking time, to allow for variations in temperature, ingredients, etc.
- Cool the cookie sheet before adding more dough. If you put cookie dough on a hot surface, it will spread too much. I place my cookie sheet outside briefly in cold weather, or place the

sheet on freezer packs on the counter.

- Remove cookies from the cookie sheet shortly after baking, or they will continue to bake. If cookies harden and stick to the cookie sheet, return to the oven for a minute. This will make cookies easier to remove.

TIPS ON STORING COOKIES

- Cool cookies completely to room temperature before sealing them in cans or plastic containers, or they will soften.

- Placing a small slice of apple in the container will keep soft cookies from drying out.

- Don't freeze cookies for longer than six weeks.

- Frozen cookies defrost quickly. For a fresh-out-of-the-oven taste and texture, place cookies on a lightly greased cookie sheet and heat in a 300° oven for about 5 to 10 minutes.

CHOCOLATE CHIP COOKIES

Makes 4 dozen

For variety, add some chopped nuts to this recipe. You may use 6 oz. of chocolate chips instead of a chocolate bar. You may also substitute whole wheat flour for 1/2 cup of the all-purpose flour.

1 cup brown sugar, packed
1/2 cup (1 stick) butter, softened
1 egg
1/2 tsp. vanilla extract

1 1/8 cups flour
1/2 tsp. baking soda
1/4 tsp. salt
6 oz. milk chocolate

Heat oven to 375°. In a medium bowl, beat sugar and butter together until creamy, then beat in egg and vanilla. In another bowl, mix flour, soda and salt. Add to creamed mixture and mix well. Chop chocolate into 1/2-inch pieces. Stir chocolate into dough. Drop by rounded teaspoon onto a greased cookie sheet. Bake for about 8 minutes, or until golden brown. Remove to racks to cool.

DELUXE OATMEAL COOKIES

Makes 5 dozen

I like dried cherries, semisweet chocolate and walnuts in these chewy cookies, but use any combination you prefer.

½ cup (1 stick) butter, softened	1 cup flour
¼ cup shortening	1 tsp. salt
½ cup granulated sugar	½ tsp. baking soda
1 cup brown sugar, packed	2 cups rolled oats
1 egg	8 oz. chocolate chips
¼ cup water	1 cup chopped dried fruit
1 tsp. vanilla extract	1 cup chopped nuts

Heat oven to 350°. Beat butter, shortening and both sugars together until creamy. Beat in egg, water and vanilla. In a separate bowl, stir together flour, salt and soda. Add to creamed mixture and beat well. Stir in oats, chocolate, fruit and nuts. Drop by rounded teaspoons onto a greased cookie sheet. Bake for 12 to 14 minutes, until golden brown. Remove to racks to cool.

MACADAMIA CHOCOLATE COOKIES

Makes 3 dozen

Chocolate and macadamia nuts are an excellent flavor combination. Use white chocolate chips for extra appeal in these cookies.

½ cup (1 stick) butter, softened
½ cup granulated sugar
¼ cup brown sugar, packed
½ tsp. vanilla extract
1 egg
1 cup flour

1 cup rolled oats
½ tsp. baking soda
¼ tsp. salt
6 oz. chocolate chips
½ cup chopped macadamia
    nuts

Heat oven to 350°. In a bowl, beat butter with both sugars until creamy. Beat in vanilla and egg. In a separate bowl, stir together flour, oats, soda and salt. Stir flour mixture into creamed mixture until blended. Add chocolate and nuts and mix well. Drop by rounded teaspoons onto a greased cookie sheet. Bake for 8 to 10 minutes, or until golden brown. Remove to racks to cool.

COCONUT CHOCOLATE MACAROONS

Makes 3 dozen

Toasting the coconut adds a nutty flavor. Regular chocolate chips are fine here, if you can't find the mini chips.

1½ cups shredded coconut
2 egg whites, room temperature
1 pinch salt

¼ cup sugar
½ cup mini chocolate chips

Heat oven to 350°. Spread coconut on an ungreased cookie sheet and toast for about 8 minutes, until golden, stirring frequently. Set aside to cool. Lower oven to 325°.

In a medium bowl, using an electric mixer, beat egg whites until foamy. Add salt and beat until soft peaks form. Gradually beat in sugar, beating until whites are very stiff and glossy. Gently fold in coconut and chocolate chips. Drop by rounded teaspoons onto a greased cookie sheet. Bake for 15 to 20 minutes, until lightly browned but still moist in the center. Remove to racks to cool.

NUTTY CHOCOLATE MACAROONS

The term "macaroon" usually refers to cookies made from ground almonds or coconut; these are an almond version.

1¼ cups almonds, toasted
1 cup sugar, divided
1 egg white
2 tbs. water
1 tbs. light corn syrup
⅓ cup unsweetened cocoa powder
confectioner's sugar

In a food processor workbowl, grind almonds with ½ cup of the sugar until finely chopped. Add egg white to mixture in workbowl and process until mixture forms a paste. Transfer to a bowl; set aside.

In a small saucepan, stir together remaining 1/2 cup sugar, water and corn syrup. Place over medium-high heat and cook until mixture is clear and reaches 240° on a candy thermometer (or forms a soft ball that flattens when removed to a plate). Set syrup aside to cool to room temperature. Heat oven to 350°.

Stir cooled syrup into almond mixture. Add cocoa and mix until blended. Drop by rounded teaspoons, 3 inches apart, onto a buttered, floured cookie sheet. Flatten tops with a moistened spoon. Sift confectioner's sugar lightly over tops of cookies.

Bake for 18 to 20 minutes, or until set. Do not overbake. Remove to racks to cool.

HAZELNUT CHOCOLATE MACAROONS

Makes 3 dozen

You can substitute whatever nuts you prefer for the hazelnuts.

3/4 cup hazelnuts
3 oz. semisweet chocolate
3 egg whites, room temperature

1 pinch salt
3/4 cup sugar
1/2 tsp. vanilla extract

Heat oven to 300°. In a food processor workbowl or blender container place hazelnuts and pulse until finely ground; set aside. Grate chocolate with a box grater or in a food processor workbowl; stir into ground nuts.

In a large bowl, using an electric mixer, beat egg whites until foamy. Add salt and beat until soft peaks form. Gradually beat in sugar, beating until stiff and glossy. Fold in nuts, chocolate and vanilla. Drop by rounded teaspoons onto a lightly greased cookie sheet. Bake for about 20 minutes, until lightly browned but still moist in the center. Remove to racks to cool.

PEANUT BUTTER COOKIES

Makes 3 dozen

For variety, try adding ¾ cup chopped peanuts or chocolate chips to the batter.

½ cup (1 stick) butter, softened
½ cup peanut butter
½ cup brown sugar, packed
1 cup granulated sugar, divided
1 egg

1 tsp. vanilla extract
1¾ cups flour
1 tsp. baking soda
½ tsp. salt

Heat oven to 375°. Beat butter, peanut butter, brown sugar and ½ cup of the granulated sugar until creamy. Beat in egg and vanilla. In a separate bowl, stir together flour, baking soda and salt. Stir into creamed mixture until well combined. Shape rounded teaspoons of dough into balls. Roll dough balls in remaining ½ cup sugar and place on a greased cookie sheet. Press the tines of a fork on each ball to flatten slightly. Bake for 10 minutes, or until golden brown. Remove to racks to cool.

OATMEAL RAISIN COOKIES

For a sweeter flavor, try replacing raisins with dried cranberries.

1/2 cup (1 stick) butter, softened
1/2 cup brown sugar, packed
1/4 cup granulated sugar
2 eggs
1 tsp. vanilla extract
1 cup flour

1/2 tsp. baking soda
1/2 tsp. salt
1 tsp. cinnamon
1 1/2 cups rolled oats
1/3 cup chopped walnuts
3/4 cup raisins

In a large bowl, beat together butter and both sugars until creamy. Beat in eggs and vanilla. In separate bowl, stir together flour, soda, salt and cinnamon. Add to creamed mixture. Stir in oats, nuts and raisins. Refrigerate for 30 minutes.

Heat oven to 350°. Drop rounded teaspoons of dough onto a greased cookie sheet, 3 inches apart. Bake for about 10 minutes, until golden brown. Remove to racks to cool.

TRADITIONAL SNICKERDOODLES

Makes 4 dozen

Snickerdoodles are a Christmastime cookie tradition and have been popular in the U.S. since the late 19th century.

2 cups sugar, divided
1/2 cup shortening
1/2 cup (1 stick) butter, softened
2 eggs
2 3/4 cups flour

1 1/2 tsp. cream of tartar
1 tsp. baking soda
1/4 tsp. salt
1 tsp. cinnamon

In a bowl, beat 1 1/2 cups of the sugar, shortening and butter together until creamy. Beat in eggs. In another bowl, stir together flour, cream of tartar, soda and salt. Add to creamed mixture and mix well. Refrigerate for 1 hour. Heat oven to 375°. Combine remaining 1/2 cup sugar and cinnamon in a bowl. Shape dough into small balls, drop into sugar mixture and coat well. Place on a greased cookie sheet and bake for about 10 minutes, until golden brown. Remove to racks to cool.

SHORTBREAD

Shortbread is an absolute classic of simplicity and taste. Each ingredient contributes to the final product. The almond and vanilla varieties will taste quite different.

1 cup (2 sticks) butter, softened
1/2 cup sugar
1/2 tsp. vanilla extract or almond extract, optional
2 1/2 cups flour
1/8 tsp. salt

In a bowl, beat butter and sugar until creamy. Add vanilla, if using. In another bowl, mix together flour and salt. Stir into creamed mixture until smooth. Refrigerate until firm. Heat oven to 300°. Divide dough in half. Pat or roll out each half into a circle about 7 inches in diameter. Place on an ungreased cookie sheet. Score each into 16 wedges. Bake for 25 to 30 minutes, until lightly browned. Cool slightly before removing from cookie sheet. Cut into wedges.

NUTTY SHORTBREAD

Make shortbread in shapes for the holidays—it's easy! These cookies can be dusted with sugar, or even frosted, if you like.

1 cup (2 sticks) butter, softened
½ cup confectioner's sugar
1 tsp. vanilla extract
2 cups flour

½ tsp. baking powder
¼ tsp. salt
1 cup finely chopped walnuts

In a bowl, beat butter and sugar together until creamy. Add vanilla, beating until light and fluffy. Sift together flour, baking powder and salt. Add to creamed mixture with nuts and stir well. Cover and refrigerate for 1 hour.

Heat oven to 350°. Roll dough out on a floured board to ¼-inch thick. Cut out shapes with a cookie cutter. Place on an ungreased cookie sheet and bake for 12 to 15 minutes, or until lightly browned. Remove immediately to racks to cool.

COCONUT MACADAMIA SHORTBREAD

Makes 4 dozen

The coconut imparts a flavor of the tropics to these rich treats.

1 cup (2 sticks) butter, softened
1/3 cup sugar
1 tsp. vanilla extract
2 cups flour
1/4 tsp. salt

3/4 cup finely chopped
  macadamia nuts
1 1/2 cups shredded coconut
1/2 cup confectioner's sugar

In a bowl, beat butter and sugar until creamy. Mix in vanilla. Add flour and salt and beat until smooth. Stir in nuts and coconut. Divide dough in half and shape into two 2-inch-thick logs. Wrap well and refrigerate until firm.

Heat oven to 350°. Cut logs into 1/4-inch slices and place on a greased cookie sheet. Bake for 10 to 12 minutes, until lightly browned. Slip a sheet of waxed paper beneath cooling racks. Transfer cookies to racks and cool for 3 to 4 minutes. Dust with confectioner's sugar. Cool completely.

GINGERSNAPS

Gingersnaps are good whether chewy or crisp: this recipe makes cookies that are crisp and delicious.

3/4 cup (1 1/2 sticks) butter,
  softened
1 1/4 cups sugar, divided
1 egg
1/4 cup molasses

2 cups flour
1 tsp. baking soda
1 tsp. cinnamon
3/4 tsp. ground cloves
1 tsp. ground ginger

Heat oven to 350°. In a bowl, beat butter and 1 cup of the sugar together until creamy. Beat in egg and molasses. In another bowl, stir together flour, soda, cinnamon, cloves and ginger. Add to creamed mixture and beat until smooth. Batter should be soft. Roll tsp. of dough into balls. Place remaining 1/4 cup sugar in a small bowl and coat balls lightly in sugar. Place on a greased cookie sheet and bake for about 10 minutes. Remove to racks to cool.

MOLASSES SPICE COOKIES

Makes: 4 dozen

The spice is distinctive but not overpowering in these addictive, chewy cookies.

1/2 cup (1 stick) butter, softened
1/4 cup shortening
1 cup granulated sugar, divided
1/2 cup brown sugar, packed
1/4 cup molasses
1 egg
2 cups flour
2 tsp. baking soda
1/4 tsp. salt
1 1/2 tsp. cinnamon, divided
3/4 tsp. ground cloves
3/4 tsp. ground ginger
1/4 tsp. ground nutmeg

Heat oven to 400°. In a bowl, beat together butter, shortening, ½ cup of the granulated sugar and brown sugar until creamy. Beat in molasses and egg.

In a separate bowl, stir together flour, soda, salt, 1 tsp. of the cinnamon, cloves, ginger and nutmeg. Add to creamed mixture and mix well. Shape rounded teaspoons of dough into balls.

In a shallow bowl, stir together remaining ½ cup of the granulated sugar with remaining ½ tsp. of the cinnamon. Roll dough balls in cinnamon sugar.

Place on a greased cookie sheet 2 inches apart and bake for 8 to 10 minutes, until golden. Remove to racks to cool.

HOLIDAY GINGERBREAD

Makes 5 dozen

These spicy holiday cookies are easy to make into shapes and decorate. You can even use them to decorate your Christmas tree.

1 tbs. light corn syrup
1 cup sugar
$1/3$ cup water
4 tsp. cinnamon
2 tsp. ground ginger
2 tsp. ground cloves
1 tsp. ground nutmeg
$1/4$ tsp. salt
$1/2$ cup (1 stick) butter, cut into pieces
$1 1/2$ tsp. baking soda
$1 1/2$ tsp. lukewarm water
1 tsp. brandy
$3–3 1/2$ cups flour

In a saucepan, mix together corn syrup, sugar, water, cinnamon, ginger, cloves, nutmeg and salt. Place over medium-high heat and cook, stirring, until sugar dissolves. Remove from heat and add butter. Stir off heat until butter is melted. Pour into a large bowl and set aside until mixture cools to room temperature.

Heat oven to 350°. Dissolve baking soda in 1½ tsp. water. Add to cooled sugar-butter mixture. Add brandy and stir well. Gradually mix in flour, adding just enough to make a stiff dough. Knead until smooth.

Roll out dough between 2 sheets of plastic wrap until ⅛-inch thick. Peel off upper wrap and cut out cookie shapes. Bake on a greased cookie sheet for 5 to 7 minutes, until cookies are deep brown in color. Remove to racks to cool.

LEMON WAFER COOKIES

I sometimes add finely chopped nuts to these delicate cookies.

1/2 cup (1 stick) butter, softened
1 cup plus 2 tsp. sugar, divided
1 1/2 tbs. grated lemon zest
1 tbs. lemon juice

2 cups flour
1/8 tsp. salt
1 tsp. baking powder

In a large bowl, beat butter and 1 cup of the sugar together until creamy. Mash remaining 2 tsp. sugar and lemon zest together in a small bowl. Stir into butter-sugar mixture along with lemon juice. In another bowl, stir together flour, salt and baking powder. Add to creamed mixture and beat well. Shape dough into 2 logs, each about 2 inches in diameter. Wrap well and refrigerate until firm.

Heat oven to 375°. Slice logs very thinly. Place slices on an ungreased cookie sheet. Bake for 8 to 10 minutes, until golden brown. Remove to racks to cool.

CARAMEL NUT WAFERS

These crisp cookies have a nice caramel flavor.

1 cup (2 sticks) butter, softened
2 cups brown sugar, packed
2 eggs
1 tsp. vanilla extract
1 tsp. baking soda

1 tsp. cream of tartar
$\frac{1}{8}$ tsp. salt
$3\frac{1}{4}$ cups flour
1 cup chopped pecans

In a bowl, beat together butter and brown sugar until light and creamy. Mix in eggs and vanilla. In another bowl, stir together soda, cream of tartar, salt and flour. Add to creamed mixture, mixing until blended. Stir in nuts. Shape dough into logs, each 2 inches in diameter. Wrap well and refrigerate until firm.

Heat oven to 350°. Cut logs into $\frac{1}{4}$-inch thick slices and place on a greased cookie sheet. Bake for 8 to 10 minutes, until golden brown. Remove to racks to cool.

BUTTERCREAM SANDWICH COOKIES

Makes 2 dozen

The wafers are delicate, contrasting nicely with the rich filling.

1 cup (2 sticks) butter, cold, cut into small pieces
2 cups flour
$\frac{1}{2}$ cup whipping cream
$\frac{1}{2}$ cup granulated sugar
$\frac{1}{4}$ cup ($\frac{1}{2}$ stick) butter, softened
1 cup confectioner's sugar
1 pinch salt
2 tsp. milk
1 tsp. vanilla extract, or $\frac{1}{2}$ tsp. almond extract
food coloring, optional

In a bowl, using a pastry cutter or a fork, cut cold butter and flour together until mixture resembles coarse crumbs. Add cream and mix until mixture forms a ball. Wrap well and refrigerate until firm.

Heat oven to 375°. On a floured board, roll out ½ of the dough at a time to ⅛-inch thick. Cut into rounds. Prick rounds with a fork. Pour granulated sugar onto a sheet of waxed paper and turn cookie rounds on waxed paper to coat completely with sugar. Place on a parchment-lined cookie sheet and bake for 8 minutes, until golden brown. Remove to racks to cool.

For filling, combine soft butter, confectioner's sugar, salt, milk, vanilla extract and food coloring (if using) in a bowl. Beat until smooth. Just before serving, spread filling on half the wafers and cover each with another wafer to form a sandwich.

HONEY-WHEAT COOKIE SANDWICHES

This crisp, pastry-like cookie is perfect with the sweet jam filling.

4 cups whole wheat flour
2 tsp. baking powder
1 cup (2 sticks) cold butter, cut
  into small pieces

1 cup honey
1 egg, beaten
$1/3$ cup hot water
$1/2$ cup raspberry jam

Heat oven to 350°. In a bowl, stir together flour and baking powder. Cut in butter with a pastry cutter or a fork until butter is pea-sized. Add honey, egg and water; mix until dough forms a ball. Roll out dough $1/4$-inch thick. Cut into circles with a cookie cutter or a glass. Place 1 inch apart on an ungreased cookie sheet. Bake for 10 to 15 minutes, or until edges are lightly browned. Remove to racks to cool. When cool, spread half of the cookies with jam and top with remaining cookies.

MINT-CHOCOLATE COOKIES

These treats are fudgy and minty at the same time.

1 cup (2 sticks) butter, softened
1 cup brown sugar, packed
$^3/_4$ cup granulated sugar
2 eggs
1 tsp. vanilla extract
$^1/_2$ tsp. peppermint extract, or more to taste

2 cups flour
$^3/_4$ cup unsweetened cocoa powder
1 tsp. baking soda
$^1/_2$ tsp. salt
8 oz. chocolate chips

Heat oven to 350°. In a bowl, beat together butter and both sugars until light and creamy. Beat in eggs, vanilla and peppermint extract. In another bowl, stir together flour, cocoa, soda and salt. Add to creamed mixture a bit at a time, mixing until blended. Stir in chocolate chips. Place rounded teaspoons of dough onto an ungreased cookie sheet. Bake for 8 to 10 minutes, until cookies are slightly cracked on top. Remove to racks to cool.

EMPANADITAS (MEXICAN TURNOVERS)

Makes 3 dozen

These are tiny, baked versions of traditional fried Mexican turnovers. They are best the day after baking, and keep well for a week.

1 cup flour
1/2 cup cornmeal
1/2 cup sugar, divided
1 1/2 tsp. baking powder
1/2 tsp. salt
3 tbs. cream cheese, softened
2 tbs. vegetable oil
6 tbs. milk, about
1/3 cup raspberry jam
1/3 cup mini chocolate chips
1/3 cup finely chopped walnuts

In a bowl mix together flour, cornmeal, ¼ cup of the sugar, baking powder and salt. Break cream cheese into small pieces and mash into flour mixture with oil until crumbly. Stir in milk 1 tbs. at a time just until dough holds together. Wrap well and refrigerate until firm.

Heat oven to 350°. In a small bowl, mix together jam, chocolate chips and nuts for the cookie filling; set aside. Set out a small bowl of water and a bowl with remaining ¼ cup sugar. Roll dough on a floured surface to ⅛ inch thick and cut into 2-inch circles. Place ½ tsp. filling in the center of each circle. Fold dough over filling and seal edges with a fork. Dip finger in water and moisten top of each cookie. Sprinkle with sugar.

Place cookies on a parchment-lined cookie sheet and bake for 12 to 15 minutes, until lightly browned. Remove to racks to cool.

GINGER CHOCOLATE THINS

Ginger adds an unexpected heat to these cookies. Find crystallized ginger in the health food or baking sections of your grocery store.

1 cup toasted hazelnuts
4 oz. bittersweet chocolate,
  grated
1/2 cup (1 stick) butter, softened
1/3 cup brown sugar, packed

1 tsp. vanilla extract
1 egg
1 cup whole wheat flour
1/3 cup minced crystallized
  ginger

In a blender container or food processor workbowl, grind nuts until fine. Transfer to a bowl and add grated chocolate. In another bowl, beat butter and sugar until creamy; beat in vanilla and egg. Add flour, nuts and chocolate. Add crystallized ginger and mix until dough is just blended. Shape into a log about 2 1/2 inches in diameter. Wrap well and refrigerate until firm. Heat oven to 350°. Slice log as thinly as possible and place on an ungreased cookie sheet. Bake for 8 minutes, until lightly browned. Remove to racks to cool.

ALMOND COINS

This recipe sounds complicated, but actually goes together quickly and easily. Be sure to line the cookie sheet with foil, as it makes removing the cookies a snap.

$\frac{1}{2}$ cup sugar
$\frac{1}{2}$ cup (1 stick) butter, softened
2 tbs. whipping cream
2 tbs. flour
1 cup finely chopped or sliced almonds

Heat oven to 350°. Place sugar, butter, cream and flour in a saucepan. Stir until blended. Place over medium-high heat and cook, stirring, until mixture comes to a boil. boil for 1 minute, stirring constantly. Remove from heat and mix in nuts. Line a cookie sheet with foil. Place dough a tsp. at a time onto foil, about 3 inches apart. Bake for 6 to 8 minutes, or until golden brown. Remove to racks to cool.

SUGAR COOKIES

It's easy to cut these cookies into shapes for holidays and special occasions. Decorate them with sprinkles if you wish.

1 cup (2 sticks) butter, softened	3$\frac{1}{2}$ cups flour
1$\frac{1}{4}$ cups sugar	1 tsp. baking powder
2 eggs	$\frac{1}{4}$ tsp. salt
1 tsp. vanilla extract	colored sugar, for garnish

In a bowl, beat butter and sugar until creamy. Beat in eggs and vanilla. In another bowl, stir together flour, baking powder and salt. Add to creamed mixture and beat well. Cover and refrigerate for 1 hour or up to overnight.

Heat oven to 400°. Roll dough $\frac{1}{8}$-inch thick on a lightly floured board. Cut into desired shapes. Place on a greased cookie sheet and sprinkle with colored sugar. Bake for 6 to 8 minutes, until lightly browned. Remove to racks to cool.

OLD-TIME SUGAR COOKIES

Makes: 5 dozen

This recipe is from the mid-1800s, and makes cookies that are perfect for decorating with colored frosting.

1/2 cup shortening	5 tsp. baking powder
1/2 cup (1 stick) butter, softened	1/2 tsp. salt
2 cups sugar	4 cups flour
3 eggs	1/2 cup milk

Heat oven to 350°. Beat together shortening, butter and sugar until creamy. Beat in eggs, 1 at a time. Stir together baking powder, salt and flour in a separate bowl. Add to creamed mixture alternately with milk, beginning and ending with flour mixture. On a lightly floured surface, roll out dough 1/4-inch thick and cut into desired shapes. Place on a greased cookie sheet. Bake for about 8 minutes until lightly browned. Remove to racks to cool.

CHOCOLATE NUT SHAPES

Makes 4 dozen

The dough for these cookies is very versatile, and can also be rolled out and cut into distinctive and festive shapes.

1 cup (2 sticks) butter, softened
2/3 cup sugar
1 egg yolk
1 tsp. vanilla extract
1/4 tsp. salt

2 1/3 cups flour
1/4 cup unsweetened cocoa
   powder
1/2 cup finely chopped almonds

Heat oven to 350°. In a bowl, beat butter and sugar together until creamy. Add egg yolk, vanilla and salt and beat until smooth. In another bowl, stir together flour and cocoa. Add to mixture and beat until smoothly blended. Stir in nuts.

Roll dough into ropes about 1/2-inch thick. Cut off 2-inch lengths and shape into crescents. Place on a lightly greased cookie sheet and bake for 8 to 10 minutes, or until set. Remove immediately to racks to cool.

WALNUT BRANDY BALLS

Makes 3 dozen

These easy-to-make balls don't need any cooking. Storing them for at least a day before eating gives time for their flavor to develop. Pecans or other nuts can be substituted for walnuts.

1 box (about 7 oz.) vanilla
   wafer cookies
2 tbs. unsweetened cocoa
1½ cups confectioner's sugar,
   divided

¼ cup brandy, rum or whiskey
1 cup finely chopped walnuts
3 tbs. light corn syrup

Break up cookies into a food processor workbowl or blender container and process to form fine crumbs. Place cookie crumbs in a bowl. Sift cocoa and 1 cup of the sugar into bowl with crumbs. Add brandy, nuts and corn syrup and mix until thoroughly combined. Shape into round balls about 1 inch in diameter and roll in remaining ½ cup sugar. Store in an airtight container for at least a day before serving.

NUTTY SNOWBALLS

Use whatever nuts you prefer in these cookies. Sometimes called Mexican wedding cakes, they are melt-in-your-mouth good. The confectioner's sugar coating gives them their name.

1/2 cup (1 stick) butter, softened
3/4 cup confectioner's sugar, divided
1 tsp. vanilla extract

1 cup flour
1/8 tsp. salt
1 cup finely chopped pecans

Heat oven to 350°. In a bowl, beat butter and 1/4 cup of the sugar until creamy. Beat in vanilla. Add flour and salt and beat until smooth. Stir in pecans.

Shape into 1-inch balls. Place on a cookie sheet and bake for 15 minutes, or until lightly browned. Remove from oven and immediately roll hot cookies in remaining 1/2 cup confectioner's sugar. When cookies are cool, roll them in sugar again.

CREAM COOKIES

Makes: 3-4 dozen

This is a very old recipe, and will become a favorite tradition in your family. The sweetened condensed milk adds a creamy richness.

1/2 cup shortening
1 1/2 cups sugar, divided
1 egg
1 tsp. baking soda
2 tsp. cream of tartar

1/2 tsp. cinnamon
1/2 tsp. salt
3/4 cup sweetened condensed milk
2 cups flour, about

Heat oven to 350°. Beat shortening and 1 cup of the sugar in a large bowl until creamy. Beat in egg, soda, cream of tartar, cinnamon, salt and condensed milk. Add enough flour to make a rollable dough. Roll dough out to about 1/2-inch thick. Cut with a round cutter. Place on a greased cookie sheet and sprinkle with remaining sugar. Bake for 8 to 10 minutes, or until golden around edges. Remove to racks to cool.

PECAN CRESCENTS

These lovely, crumbly cookies are loaded with sweet pecans.

1/4 cup sweetened condensed milk
1/2 cup (1 stick) butter, softened
1/2 tsp. vanilla extract
1 1/2 cups flour

3/4 cup confectioners' sugar, divided
1/2 tsp. salt
1 cup finely chopped pecans

In a large bowl, beat together condensed milk, butter and vanilla. Sift together flour, 1/2 cup of the sugar and salt. Stir into butter mixture until well mixed; fold in pecans. Wrap dough and refrigerate for at least 1 hour. Heat oven to 375°. Roll walnut-sized pieces of dough into fat cylinders and form in crescent shapes. Arrange cookies on a foil-lined cookie sheet. Bake for 12 minutes until set; do not brown. Cool cookies for 1 minute on cookie sheet. While still warm, roll cookies in remaining 1/4 cup confectioner's sugar.

CHOCOLATE ORANGE FINGERS

Makes 4 dozen

Chocolate and orange complement each other beautifully.

1/2 cup (1 stick) butter, softened
1/2 cup sugar
1 egg yolk
2 tbs. frozen orange juice
  concentrate, thawed

1 tbs. grated orange zest
1 1/2 cups flour
1/2 tsp. baking powder
6 oz. semisweet chocolate chips

In a bowl, beat butter and sugar until creamy. Beat in egg yolk, juice concentrate and zest. In another bowl, mix flour and baking powder. Add to creamed mixture and mix well. Refrigerate until firm. Heat oven to 350°. Roll dough into 1/4-inch-thick ropes and cut into 2-inch fingers. Place on a greased cookie sheet. Bake for 8 to 10 minutes, until golden brown. Remove to wire racks and cool.

Melt chocolate in a small bowl in the microwave on high power. Dip each cookie halfway into melted chocolate. Place dipped cookies on a foil-lined pan and refrigerate until firm.

CHOCOLATE NUT FINGERS

Makes 4 dozen

Chocolate cookies dipped in chocolate — what could be more decadent? Use your favorite nuts for dipping.

3/4 cup (1 1/2 sticks) butter, softened
3/4 cup brown sugar, packed
1 1/4 cups flour

1/4 cup unsweetened cocoa
1/4 tsp. salt
6 oz. semisweet chocolate chips
1/2 cup finely chopped nuts

In a bowl, beat butter and sugar until creamy. In another bowl, stir together flour, cocoa and salt. Add to creamed mixture and mix well. Refrigerate until firm. Heat oven to 325°. On a lightly floured board, roll dough into 1/4-inch-thick ropes and cut into 2-inch fingers. Place on a greased cookie sheet and bake for 15 minutes, or until set. Remove to wire racks and cool. Melt chocolate in a small bowl in the microwave on high. Dip each cookie halfway into melted chocolate and immediately roll in nuts. Place dipped cookies on a foil-lined pan and refrigerate until firm.

SESAME SEED TWISTS

These plain cookies, called koulourakia, are a Greek tradition.

1/2 cup (1 stick) butter, softened
2/3 cup sugar
3 egg yolks, divided
3 tbs. half-and-half
1 tsp. vanilla extract

2 cups flour
1/4 tsp. cinnamon
1 tsp. baking powder
1 tsp. water
1/4 cup sesame seeds

Heat oven to 350°. Beat butter and sugar together until creamy. Add 2 of the egg yolks, half-and-half and vanilla and mix well. In another bowl, mix flour, cinnamon and baking powder. Add to creamed mixture and mix well. Cover and refrigerate for 1 hour.

Beat remaining egg yolk with water in a small bowl. Roll small balls of dough on a floured board into thin 6-inch-long strands. Fold each strand fold in half and twist gently to create a spiral. Place on a greased cookie sheet, brush with yolk and sprinkle with sesame seeds. Bake for 12 to 15 minutes. Remove to racks to cool.

ALMOND TUILES

Makes: 2 dozen

Also called lace cookies, these beauties are easy and so elegant. If the cookies firm up too quickly to mold into shape, pop them back into a warm oven for 30 seconds. Bake only 3 or 4 cookies at a time, since you need to shape each one while it's still hot.

1/4 cup (1/2 stick) butter, softened
1/2 cup sugar
2 egg whites
1/4 cup cake flour
1/4 tsp. vanilla extract
1/3 cup finely ground almonds
1/2 cup sliced almonds

Heat oven to 425°. Beat butter and sugar together in a bowl until light and creamy. Add egg whites and beat until smooth. Add flour and vanilla, beating until blended. Stir in ground almonds.

Drop batter by scant tsp. onto a greased cookie sheet, placing at least 4 inches apart. Spread into roughly 3-inch circles with the back of a spoon. Batter will appear thin and open in spots. Sprinkle each cookie with a few sliced almonds.

Bake for 4 minutes, or until lightly browned. Remove from oven; immediately remove each cookie from cookie sheet and drape over a wooden dowel or slender rolling pin. When cool, remove to a rack. (You may also drape hot cookies over inverted small bowls, to create tuile cups.)

Store in an airtight container. If left uncovered, these cookies will become limp.

KRUMKAKE

In Denmark, these are called krum kager; *they're similar to Italian pizzelles, in that they are a thin wafer-like cookie baked on a special iron on the stove.They can be served flat, straight off the krumkake iron, or rolled into tubes or cones and filled with whipped cream or ice cream.*

1 cup whipping cream
1 cup sugar
4 eggs
1¼ cups flour
1 tsp. grated lemon zest
melted butter

Place cream in a bowl and gradually beat in sugar, mixing just to dissolve sugar, not to whip the cream. Beat eggs in a separate bowl with an electric mixer until thick and light. Fold into cream mixture. Gently but thoroughly fold in flour and lemon zest. Heat a krumkake iron on medium heat on the stove until hot. Brush surface with melted butter. Pour 1 tbs. batter over iron. Bake until golden brown, about 1 to 2 minutes each side. Lift cookie from iron and immediately roll around a wooden spoon handle or shape into a cone. Set on a rack to cool completely. Repeat with remaining batter.

CARAMEL CRUNCH COOKIES

This is a rich, chewy cookie with a surprising sparkle of caramel.

1 cup sugar to caramelize
1 cup (2 sticks) butter, softened
$1/3$ cup granulated sugar
$1/3$ cup brown sugar, packed
1 tsp. vanilla extract
$1^2/3$ cups flour
$3/4$ tsp. baking powder
2 tbs. water

First caramelize 1 cup of sugar. Spread sugar evenly in the bottom of a heavy pan. Place over medium heat and shake pan without stirring until sugar melts and caramelizes. Sugar can go from barely golden to burnt very quickly, so watch carefully, or you may have to throw out your first attempt and begin again!

As soon as sugar is a golden brown, immediately pour it onto a cookie sheet lined with buttered foil. Cool completely. When hard, remove from foil and chop caramel into small pieces. Set aside.

For dough, first heat oven to 325°.

In a bowl, beat butter and both sugars together until creamy. Add vanilla. In a separate bowl, stir together flour and baking powder. Add half the flour mixture to the creamed mixture, then stir in the water, then the remaining flour mixture. Stir in crushed caramelized sugar.

Drop dough by rounded teaspoons onto a well-greased cookie sheet. Bake for 12 minutes, or until lightly browned. Cool 1 minute on cookie sheet, then remove to racks to cool completely.

VANILLA CRESCENTS

Store vanilla sugar in your pantry where it will keep for at least a month. Use it any time confectioner's sugar is called for. Plain confectioner's sugar is fine in this recipe, if you can't find vanilla beans.

1 vanilla bean
1 lb. confectioner's sugar
2 cups flour

1 cup (2 sticks) butter, softened
1¼ cups finely ground almonds

Split vanilla bean lengthwise; scrape seeds into sugar. Cut bean into 2-inch pieces and stir into sugar. Place in a tightly sealed container and set aside for at least 1 day before making cookies.

Heat oven to 350°. In a bowl, mix flour, butter and ½ cup of the vanilla sugar until crumbly. Add nuts and stir well. Roll tsp. of dough into balls and shape each into a crescent. Place on an ungreased cookie sheet and bake for 10 to 12 minutes, until lightly browned. While still warm, roll in vanilla sugar.

CINNAMON-NUT PALMIERS

These cookies look fancy, but are a breeze to make. Find puff pastry in the freezer section of your grocery store.

½ cup sugar	1 lb. (2 sheets) puff pastry,
2 tsp. cinnamon	thawed
½ cup finely chopped walnuts	1 egg, beaten

In a small bowl, stir together sugar, cinnamon and nuts; set aside. On a floured surface, gently roll 1 sheet of puff pastry to about an 11-inch square. Sprinkle with ½ the sugar-nut mixture. Gently roll 1 side of pastry toward the center. Repeat with opposite side, with both rolls meeting in the center. Repeat with remaining pastry sheet and filling. Wrap well and refrigerate until firm. Heat oven to 400°. Slice rolls ¼-inch thick. Place slices cut side down on a parchment-lined cookie sheet and bake for 15 minutes, until well browned on the bottom. Flip cookies and bake 5 to 10 minutes longer, until well browned. Remove to racks to cool.

FLORENTINES

These thin candy-like confections spread while baking, so allow plenty of room between cookies on the cookie sheet.

3 tbs. plus 1 tsp. butter, divided
1/2 cup whipping cream
2/3 cup sugar
1 1/2 cups sliced almonds
2 tbs. minced candied ginger

1/4 cup minced candied orange
   zest, optional
1/2 cup flour
8 oz. semisweet chocolate chips

Heat oven to 350°. Place 3 tbs. of the butter, cream and sugar in a medium saucepan over medium heat and bring to a boil, stirring constantly. Remove from heat and stir in almonds, ginger, zest (if using) and flour. Drop by rounded teaspoons onto a cookie sheet and spread out slightly. Bake for 10 minutes, or until bottoms are light brown. Cool on a rack. Melt chocolate with remaining 1 tsp. butter in the microwave. Stir until smooth; spread chocolate on the flat underside of each cookie. Cool cookies chocolate-side up.

BIZCOCHITOS

These delicate cinnamon-anise cookies can be made with your favorite cookie cutters. They are better the day after baking.

1 cup shortening	1/2 tsp. baking powder
1 cup sugar, divided	1/2 tsp. salt
1 tsp. anise seed	1/4 cup brandy
1 egg	1/2 tsp. cinnamon
3 cups flour	

Heat oven to 350°. In a bowl, beat shortening and 3/4 cup of the sugar until creamy. Add anise seed and beat until fluffy. Stir in egg. In a separate bowl, stir flour with baking powder and salt. Stir into creamed mixture along with brandy. On a floured surface, roll dough out 1/4-inch thick and cut into squares. In a small bowl, combine remaining 1/4 cup sugar and cinnamon; sprinkle over tops of cookies. Place on a greased cookie sheet and bake for 10 minutes, or until bottoms are lightly brown. Remove to racks to cool.

HONEY-ORANGE COOKIES

Makes: 2½ dozen

Orange, honey and a hint of spice combine for a rich, unusual treat. These are even better a few days after baking.

¾ cup (1½ sticks) butter, softened
1 cup sugar
2 egg yolks, divided
1½ tsp. grated orange zest

¼ cup honey
2¼ cups flour
2 tsp. baking powder
½ tsp. salt
½ tsp. ground nutmeg

Heat oven to 350°. In a bowl, beat butter and sugar until creamy. Beat in 1 of the egg yolks, zest and honey. In a separate bowl stir together flour, baking powder, salt and nutmeg; stir into the creamed mixture. Place rounded tsp. of dough about 2 inches apart onto a greased cookie sheet. Flatten cookies slightly with a fork. Brush with remaining egg yolk. Bake for 10 minutes, or until golden around edges. Remove to racks to cool.

CARROT-RAISIN COOKIES

Makes 2 dozen

Chopped nuts or a bit of shredded coconut are also wonderful additions to these moist, flavorful bites.

¾ cup (1½ sticks) butter, softened
½ cup honey
1 egg
1 tsp. vanilla extract
½ tsp. grated orange zest

2 cups flour
2 tsp. baking powder
½ tsp. salt
1¼ cups grated carrots
½ cup raisins

Heat oven to 375°. In a bowl, beat butter and honey until creamy. Add egg and beat well. Stir in vanilla and zest. In a separate bowl, stir together flour, baking powder and salt. Stir dry ingredients into creamed mixture ⅓ at a time. Stir in carrots. Drop rounded tsp. of dough 2 inches apart on a greased cookie sheet. Bake for 15 minutes. Remove to racks to cool.

PUMPKIN CRANBERRY COOKIES

Makes 3 dozen

These moist, spicy cookies are not just for Halloween. Remember to use plain pureed pumpkin, not pumpkin pie filling.

1 cup canned pumpkin puree
3/4 cup brown sugar, packed
2 tbs. honey
1/2 cup vegetable oil
1 tsp. vanilla extract
2 cups flour
1 tsp. baking powder

1 tsp. baking soda
1/2 tsp. salt
1 tsp. cinnamon
1/2 tsp. ground nutmeg
1/4 tsp. ground ginger
1 cup chopped dried cranberries
1/2 cup chopped walnuts

Heat oven to 350°. Beat pumpkin, brown sugar, honey, oil and vanilla in a bowl until blended. In another bowl, stir together flour, baking powder, soda, salt, cinnamon, nutmeg and ginger. Add dry ingredients to pumpkin mixture and mix well. Stir in cranberries and nuts. Drop by rounded tsp. onto a greased cookie sheet. Bake for 12 to 15 minutes, until golden brown. Remove to racks to cool.

ZUCCHINI DROP COOKIES

Makes: 2 dozen

What a delicious way to use those leftover zucchini in the summer! These are somewhat reminiscent of carrot cake.

½ cup (1 stick) butter, softened
1 cup sugar
1 egg
1 cup grated zucchini
1 tsp. grated lemon zest
2 cups flour

1 tsp. baking soda
1 tsp. cinnamon
½ tsp. ground cloves
½ tsp. salt
1 cup raisins

Heat oven to 375°. In a bowl, beat butter and sugar until creamy. Beat in egg, then zucchini and zest. Sift together flour, soda, cinnamon, cloves and salt. Add to zucchini mixture. Stir in raisins. Drop by rounded tsp. 2 inches apart on a greased cookie sheet. Bake for 12 to 15 minutes, until brown around edges. Remove to racks to cool.

RAISIN NUT CHEWS

These chews are simply fruit and nuts held together with a caramel-like batter. It is easy to substitute different kinds of dried fruit for the raisins, and almost any combination of nuts will also work well — use all your favorites.

1¼ cups raisins, coarsely chopped
8 oz. pitted dates, chopped (about 1¼ cups)
3 cups coarsely chopped mixed nuts
1¼ cups flour, divided
½ cup (1 stick) butter, softened
¾ cup brown sugar, packed
1 egg
½ tsp. baking soda
½ tsp. baking powder
¾ tsp. cinnamon
¼ tsp. salt

Heat oven to 350°. In a bowl, mix raisins, dates and nuts with ¼ cup of the flour. Stir to coat and set aside.

In another bowl, beat butter and brown sugar together until light and creamy. Beat in egg. Sift remaining 1 cup flour with baking soda, baking powder, cinnamon and salt. Add dry ingredients to creamed mixture and beat until smooth. Stir in fruit and nut mixture.

Place by rounded tsp. onto a greased cookie sheet. Bake for 10 to 12 minutes, until lightly browned. Remove to racks to cool.

COBWEB COOKIES

These cookies are perfect for Halloween, but the kids will want them any time of the year.

³/₄ cup flour
½ cup sugar
¼ cup vegetable oil
¼ cup milk
½ tsp. vanilla extract
2 eggs
butter for skillet
confectioner's sugar

Heat oven to 325°. Beat flour, sugar, oil, milk, vanilla and eggs in a medium bowl with an electric mixer on medium speed until smooth. Pour batter into a plastic squeeze bottle with a narrow opening, or in a locking plastic bag, and snip off one small corner.

Heat a small skillet over medium heat until hot; grease lightly. For each cookie, working quickly, squeeze batter to form 4 straight, thin lines that cross in the center form a star shape. Quickly squeeze thin streams of batter to connect lines, forming a cobweb.

Cook for 30 seconds to 1 minute just until bottoms are golden brown; carefully turn. Cook until golden brown on second side; remove from skillet. Cool on a wire rack. Continue with remaining batter. Bake cookies on ungreased cookie sheet 5 to 7 minutes or until almost crisp. Remove to racks to cool and become crisp. Sprinkle with confectioner's sugar. Store cookies in container with loose-fitting cover.

CHOCOLATE DATE COOKIES

Makes 4 dozen

These soft chocolate cookies are extra-moist because of the dates. However, you can use 6 oz. chocolate chips instead of dates if you wish, or add walnuts.

1/2 cup (1 stick) butter, softened
1 cup brown sugar, packed
2 oz. unsweetened chocolate, melted
1 egg
1/3 cup milk

1 2/3 cups flour
1 tsp. baking powder
1/4 tsp. baking soda
1 cup chopped dates
Chocolate Frosting, follows, optional

Heat oven to 375°. Beat butter and brown sugar together until creamy. Beat in melted chocolate and egg. Add milk and mix well. In a separate bowl, stir together flour, baking powder and soda. Add to creamed mixture. Stir in dates.

Drop by rounded tsp. onto a greased cookie sheet. Bake for 8 to 10 minutes, or until set. Immediately remove to wire racks to cool. If desired, frost with *Chocolate Frosting*.

CHOCOLATE FROSTING
2 tbs. butter
2 oz. unsweetened chocolate
2 cups confectioner's sugar
3 tbs. water, about

In a medium bowl, microwave butter and chocolate on high until melted, checking and stirring every 30 seconds to avoid burning. Stir in confectioner's sugar. Add enough water to make the mixture spreading consistency.

MAPLE WALNUT COOKIES

Makes: 1 dozen

These sweet treats are delicious any time of year.

³/₄ cup (1¹/₂ sticks) butter,
    softened
1 cup brown sugar, packed
1 tsp. maple extract
¹/₂ tsp. vanilla extract

1 egg
1¹/₂ cups flour
1 tsp. baking soda
¹/₂ tsp. salt
¹/₂ cup chopped walnuts

Heat oven to 350°. In a bowl, beat butter and brown sugar until creamy. Beat in maple and vanilla extracts and egg. In a small bowl, combine flour, soda and salt. Stir into creamed mixture. (The dough will be very sticky.) Stir in walnuts. Drop by tsp. onto a greased cookie sheet. Bake for 10 to 12 minutes. Rest for 1 minute; remove cookies to a rack to cool.

CHOCOLATE CINNAMON BISCOTTI

Makes 3 dozen

Biscotti means "twice-cooked." They are dry, long-lasting cookies.

1 tsp. vanilla extract
3 eggs
2 cups flour
3/4 cup sugar
3 tbs. unsweetened cocoa

2 tsp. cinnamon
1 tsp. baking soda
1/2 tsp. salt
3/4 cup toasted, chopped almonds

Heat oven to 350°. In a bowl, beat vanilla and eggs until light and thick. In another bowl, combine flour, sugar, cocoa, cinnamon, soda and salt. Add egg mixture and mix until blended, about 1 minute. Add almonds to mixture. Divide dough in half. Form dough into 2 logs about 12 inches long each on a greased cookie sheet. Bake for 25 minutes, until cooked through. Cool on a wire rack for 5 to 10 minutes. Reduce oven to 250°. Cut logs diagonally into 1/2-inch-thick slices. Lay slices flat on cookie sheet and cook for 10 minutes. Remove to racks to cool. Store tightly covered.

ITALIAN BISCOTTI

Anise, the traditional flavoring for Italian biscotti, comes from a Mediterranean herb and is similar in flavor to licorice.

$1/2$ cup (1 stick) butter, softened	3 cups flour
1 cup sugar	$1\frac{1}{2}$ tsp. baking powder
3 eggs	$1/2$ tsp. salt
2 tsp. anise seed, lightly crushed	$3/4$ cup chopped almonds

Heat oven to 350°. In a bowl, beat butter and sugar together until creamy. Add eggs and beat in well. Beat in anise. In another bowl, stir together flour, baking powder and salt. Add to creamed mixture and beat until smooth. Stir in nuts. Divide dough in half. Form dough into 2 logs about 12 inches long each on a greased cookie sheet. Bake for 25 minutes, until cooked through. Cool on a wire rack for 5 to 10 minutes. Reduce oven to 250°. Cut logs diagonally into $1/2$-inch-thick slices. Lay slices flat on cookie sheet and cook for 10 minutes. Remove to racks to cool. Store tightly covered.

RED-AND-GREEN BISCOTTI

Makes 3 dozen

Cherries and pistachios add holiday colors to these cookies.

$1/3$ cup butter, softened	$2 1/4$ cups flour
$3/4$ cup sugar	$1 1/2$ tsp. baking powder
2 eggs	$1/2$ tsp. salt
1 tsp. vanilla extract	1 cup chopped dried cherries
1 tsp. grated lemon zest	$3/4$ cup shelled pistachio nuts

Heat oven to 350°. In a bowl, beat butter and sugar until creamy. Beat in eggs, vanilla and zest. In another bowl, combine flour, baking powder and salt. Add to creamed mixture and blend. Add cranberries and nuts and mix. Divide dough in half. Form dough into 2 logs about 12 inches long each on a greased cookie sheet. Bake for 25 minutes, until cooked through. Cool on a wire rack for 5 to 10 minutes. Reduce oven to 250°. Cut logs diagonally into $1/2$-inch-thick slices. Lay slices flat on cookie sheet and cook for 10 minutes. Remove to racks to cool. Store tightly covered.

CHOCOLATE-NUT TOFFEE BARS

Makes 3 dozen

Cut these bars into small pieces — with a toffee shortbread crust and chocolate, fruit and nuts on top, they are a serious mouthful!

1 cup (2 sticks) butter, softened
1 cup brown sugar, packed
1 egg yolk
1/2 tsp. almond extract
2 cups flour

1/4 tsp. salt
8 oz. semisweet chocolate chips
3/4 cup sliced almonds
3/4 cup chopped dried apricots

Heat oven to 350°. Beat butter and brown sugar in a bowl until creamy; beat in egg yolk and extract. Stir in flour and salt until dough is well combined. Press evenly in a 9 x 13-inch baking pan. Bake for 20 to 25 minutes or until lightly browned. Immediately sprinkle chocolate chips over hot crust, spreading as they melt. While chocolate is still hot, sprinkle on almonds and apricots, pressing lightly to adhere. Cool completely before cutting into bars.

CLASSIC SEVEN-LAYER BARS

Makes 3 dozen

These are incredibly fast to make, and are always a big hit. An added bonus: it's a one-pan recipe, with no bowls to wash!

1 cup (1 stick) butter	8 oz. semisweet chocolate chips
1 cup graham cracker crumbs	1 can (14 oz.) sweetened
1 cup shredded coconut	condensed milk
8 oz. butterscotch chips	6 cups chopped walnuts

Heat oven to 350°. Cut butter into pieces and place in a 9 x 13-inch baking pan. Place in the oven for a few minutes to melt butter. Remove pan and swirl to coat bottom of pan with butter. Sprinkle graham cracker crumbs over melted butter. Sprinkle coconut over cracker crumbs, butterscotch chips over coconut, and chocolate chips over butterscotch chips. Pour sweetened condensed milk over ingredients in pan. Spread nuts on top. Bake for 30 to 35 minutes. Cool completely in the pan before cutting into small bars.

TRADITIONAL LEMON BARS

Use fresh lemons for the best flavor in these delectable bars.

1 cup (2 sticks) cold butter, cut into small pieces
2¼ cups flour, divided
¾ cup confectioner's sugar, divided
4 eggs
1½ cups granulated sugar
1 tsp. baking powder
½ tsp. salt
⅓ cup lemon juice
2 tbs. grated lemon zest

Heat oven to 350°. Cut butter into 2 cups of the flour and 1/2 cup of the confectioner's sugar until crumbly. Press mixture into the bottom and about 1 inch up the sides of a buttered 9 x 13-inch pan. Bake for 15 to 20 minutes, until lightly browned.

Leave oven at 350°. Beat eggs in a large bowl. In a separate bowl, stir together granulated sugar, remaining 1/4 cup flour baking powder and salt. Beat flour mixture into eggs until smooth. Beat in lemon juice and zest until well combined and pour into crust. Bake for 25 to 30 minutes, until filling is just set. Sprinkle with remaining 1/4 cup confectioner's sugar while hot. Cool completely in pan before cutting into bars.

CRISPY PEANUT BUTTER BARS

Makes 2 dozen

These are like their famous cousins, Rice Crispy bars, but dressed up with peanut butter and chocolate.

1 cup light corn syrup
$^3/_4$ cup granulated sugar
$^1/_4$ cup brown sugar, packed

1 cup creamy peanut butter
6 cups crisp rice cereal
8 oz. semisweet chocolate chips

Place corn syrup and both sugars in a large saucepan over medium-high heat. Bring to a boil, reduce heat to low and simmer for 1 minute, or until sugar is completely dissolved. Remove from heat and stir in peanut butter, then cereal until well combined. Stir in chocolate chips. Press evenly in a greased 9 x 13-inch baking pan. Cool completely before cutting into small bars.

DATE-COCONUT CHEWS

Makes 2 dozen

It is easy to vary this recipe with other dried fruits of your choice. You can also use vary the nuts according to your taste.

1/2 cup chopped dried apricots
1 cup chopped pitted dates
3/4 cup chopped dried figs
1 cup chopped pecans or walnuts
2 1/2 cups shredded coconut, divided
1 tbs. orange juice concentrate, thawed
1 egg, beaten

Heat oven to 350°. In a bowl, mix apricots, pecans, dates, 1 1/2 cups of the coconut and orange juice concentrate. Add egg and stir until blended. Shape dough into short logs about 1/2-inch thick. Roll in remaining coconut.

Place on a greased cookie sheet and bake for 10 to 15 minutes, until lightly browned. Remove to racks to cool.

CHOCOLATE-COCONUT BITES

These confections need no baking and take moments to prepare.

1/2 cup butter
2 cups sugar
1/2 cup whole milk (not skim or low-fat)
3 tbs. unsweetened cocoa powder
1/2 tsp. instant coffee granules dissolved in 1 tsp. hot water
3 cups rolled oats
1/2 cup shredded coconut

In a large saucepan over medium heat, combine butter, sugar and milk. Bring to a boil, stirring occasionally; boil for 4 to 5 minutes.

Remove from heat and stir in cocoa until well combined. Stir in coffee mixture, oats and coconut. Spoon by rounded tsp. onto waxed paper and set aside to cool until firm. Store in an airtight container.

CRANBERRY CHOCOLATE CLUSTERS

Tangy cranberries are balanced by sweet chocolate and the crunch of nuts in these easy, elegant clusters. Try using dried cherries and pecans, or chopped dried apricots and almonds as well. Do use the best quality chocolate in this recipe.

2 cups chocolate chips (any type)
$\frac{1}{2}$ tsp. butter
$\frac{2}{3}$ cup dried cranberries
$\frac{2}{3}$ cup chopped pecans

In a glass bowl, heat chocolate with butter on high, checking and stirring every 30 seconds, until just melted. Stir in cranberries and pecans. Spoon by rounded tsp. onto waxed paper and set aside to cool until firm. Store in an airtight container.

INDEX